St. Paul

Scott
Hahn

Our Sunday Visitor Publishing Division
Our Sunday Visitor, Inc.
Huntington, Indiana 46750

Table of Contents

Trying to write *A Pocket Guide to St. Paul* is more than a little like writing *A Pocket Guide to Nuclear Physics* or *A Pocket Guide to Neurosurgery*. St. Paul is the most influential writer in the history of literature. His work comprises a significant portion of the most influential book in all human history. His erudition was vast, his thought complex, and his accomplishments prodigious. For the magnitude of his effect on the course of human events, he has no rival except his master, Jesus Christ, whose Gospel St. Paul served and proclaimed.

Yet here we are, trying to fit St. Paul in our pockets!

Early Christian historians tell us that the Apostle Paul was indeed small of stature, perhaps little more than five feet tall. Nevertheless, he stands before us as a giant. The achievements of Alexander the Great, Caesar

Augustus, William Shakespeare, Albert Einstein — grand as they are — seem small when compared to the achievements of St. Paul. C. S. Lewis imagined that an encounter with St. Paul, even in heaven, would be "rather an overwhelming experience." He recalled that "when Dante saw the great apostles in heaven they affected him like mountains."

Paul had singular gifts. Some scholars argue that, if he had gone into philosophy, he would have surpassed Plato and Aristotle. But he was not merely a thinker. He was a pastor as well, and a missionary. He traveled far and wide to win souls. He negotiated for the peace of the Church. He corrected and encouraged people. He preached and he wrote with passion and wit. He suffered much, and ultimately, he died for the cause.

He aimed to extend the reach of Christianity through all the western lands of the Roman Empire. And he succeeded to an astonishing degree. By the end of his life — and largely thanks to his efforts — Christianity enjoyed a worldwide presence. Within a century —

largely due to the momentum of Paul's preaching — the Church had grown so large that it was perceived as a threat to the Roman social order. Less than three centuries after Paul's martyrdom, Rome was a Christian city at the head of a Christian empire.

That was his first revolution, but not his last. He has emerged repeatedly down the millennia as a fresh voice, compelling preachers, rulers, and ordinary Christians to envision a new way of living. In the fifth century, St. Augustine re-thought the world along lines that he discerned in St. Paul. In the 16th century, Paul's letters were at the center of the controversies of the Protestant Reformation and the Catholic Counter-Reformation — controversies that reshaped the world.

It's hard to exaggerate St. Paul's importance, though some people do. He was not the "founder of Christianity" or its "inventor," as a few scholars contend. Christ himself founded the Church, and he founded it on another Apostle: St. Peter. But Christ did call Saul of Tarsus and commissioned him to receive the Gospel and take it to the world. Paul gratefully acknowledged his debt not only to Jesus, but to the Apostles Peter, James, and John (see Gal 1:18; 2:9). So, though Paul did not found *the Church* of Jesus Christ, he founded many churches in Jesus' name.

But, uniquely inspired by God, he developed a theology of the Church that was authoritative. The Church's self-understanding is dependent upon the words of St. Paul. Every Christian's self-understanding should be, too. We cannot understand Christianity unless we understand his message. We cannot understand ourselves as Christians unless we see ourselves in the light of his letters.

1. How We Know About St. Paul

The New Testament is our richest, most ancient, and most reliable source of information about St. Paul. Of its 27 books, 13 are letters attributed to St. Paul. (Many Church Fathers, and a small but growing number of modern scholars, credit him with a 14th letter as well, the Letter to the Hebrews.)

In addition to those more direct sources, we find a detailed account of St. Paul's travels in the Acts of the Apostles, which was written by St. Luke, one of the Apostle's traveling companions (see 2 Tim 4:11; Philem 24). The Second Letter of Peter also gives us brief but valuable observations about Paul. In just two verses, Peter manages to confirm the authority and office of his fellow Apostle. He describes Paul as a "beloved brother," rich in wisdom, and he discusses Paul's writings explicitly as "Scriptures" — though he acknowledges that "there are some things in them hard to understand" (2 Pet 3:15-16). A final New Testament witness is St. Luke's Gospel, which was surely influenced by Paul. Thus, well over half the New Testament bears some testimony to the life and doctrine of Paul.

Paul's influence was immediate, profound, and widespread. All of the writers of the generation after his own — the Apostolic Fathers — show a familiarity with his work. Many quote him directly.

In the 2,000 years since St. Paul's martyrdom, Christians have produced many commentaries on him. In my own library, I have more than a thousand such books — and they are but a small fraction of the works in print! And the works in print are a still smaller fraction of the works that have vanished from memory. Yet Paul's life and work still hold Christians spellbound — and theological reflection produces new insights even today. His teaching is an inexhaustible treasury.

2. St. Paul's Life

Early Life

St. Paul was born, probably in the first decade of the first century A.D., in the city of Tarsus, in the Roman province of Syria-Cilicia (on what is now the southeastern coast of Turkey). Tarsus was a metropolis, a center of commerce and education. Paul was born into a devout Jewish family, but he was born a Roman citizen (Acts 22:28), a rare privilege, not easily attained in the provinces. *Saul* was the name he used among his fellow Jews; *Paul* was his Roman name. As a child, he apparently received an excellent education in Greek culture, evident in his preaching and writing (Acts 17:28, for example).

He must have been a very gifted child, for at adolescence he was sent to distant Jerusalem to study at the feet of the greatest living teacher. Gamaliel I, known as "the Great," was the first Jewish teacher to be addressed not as *rabbi* ("my master") but *rabban* ("our master"). So great was his renown that the Mishna, an ancient collection of Jewish commentary, declared: "When Rabban Gamaliel the Elder died, the glory of the Torah ceased, and purity and piety perished."

As a student of Gamaliel, Saul memorized the Scriptures — entire books at a time. He studied deeply in the Law and the prophets to discern God's plan for the Chosen People. Looking back on his school days, he recalled that he was "educated according to the strict manner of the law of our fathers" and "zealous for God" (Acts 22:3). He identified himself as a Pharisee (Acts 23:6). The Pharisees were a lay movement in Judaism, devoted to careful study and observance of the Law of Israel. They appear often in the Gospels as Jesus' antagonists. They laid the foundations for future rabbinic Judaism — that is, Judaism as we know it today.

Saul the Persecutor
Saul and the Pharisees were indeed zealous for the Law. They wished to enforce its strict

observance so that they might hasten the day when God would restore to Israel the kingdom of David. Like many Jews of his time, Paul awaited the *Messiah* — in Greek, the word is *Christos*; in English, "anointed one" or "Christ" — who would deliver the Jews from foreign oppression.

Yet Saul persecuted those Jews who proclaimed *Jesus* as the Christ (see Phil 3:5-6). He thought they were abandoning the God of their ancestors in order to worship a man — a man who proclaimed himself equal to God (Jn 5:18) and who died under a curse, according to the Law of Moses (Deut 21:23). That man, moreover, had sought to undermine obedience to Jewish customs, such as Sabbath observance (Mt 12:12), worship at the Temple in Jerusalem (Jn 4:21), and strict limitations on table fellowship (Lk 5:30).

As a "young man" (Acts 7:58) — probably in his late 20s or early 30s — Saul consented to the bloody execution of the first martyr, the deacon St. Stephen (Acts 8:1). Afterward, he went about ravaging the Church, and "entering house after house, he dragged off men and women and committed them to prison" (Acts 8:3), "breathing threats and murder against the disciples of the Lord" (Acts 9:1). Saul was caught up in the wave of religiously motivated violence that would, in a few decades, become a full-scale war of rebellion against Rome. He would one day confess: "I persecuted the church of God violently and tried to destroy it; and I advanced in Judaism beyond many of my own age among my people, so extremely zealous was I for the traditions of my fathers" (Gal 1:13-14).

In his violent zeal, Saul serves as a vivid illustration of Jesus' prophecy to his disciples: "They will put you out of the synagogues; indeed, the hour is coming when whoever kills you will think he is offering service to God. And they will do this because they have not known the Father, nor me" (Jn 16:2-3).

Call and Conversion
Saul was about to take his show on the road. From the high priest in Jerusalem he obtained

papers authorizing him to go to the synagogues of Damascus and round up followers
of Jesus so that "he might bring them bound"
(Acts 9:2) back to the holy city for prose-
cution.

But while he was approaching Damascus,
a strange thing happened. The story is so
important for our understanding of early
Christian history that it appears three times in
the Acts of the Apostles (in chapters 9, 22, and
26). First, "a light from heaven flashed" before
Saul, and "he fell to the ground and heard a
voice saying to him, 'Saul, Saul, why do you
persecute me?'"

Saul asked, "Who are you, Lord?"

And the voice answered, "I am Jesus,
whom you are persecuting" (Acts 9:3-5).

The voice commanded Saul to go on to
Damascus, where he would receive further
instructions. Meanwhile, in the city, the Lord
commanded a believer named Ananias to find
Saul and heal him. Ananias, however, knew
Saul by reputation and feared him. But the
Lord reassured him: "Go, for [Saul] is a

chosen instrument of mine to carry my name before the Gentiles and kings and the sons of Israel" (Acts 9:15).

Saul was, in short order, healed, baptized, and welcomed into the community of believers.

Ever afterward, the "Road to Damascus" has served as shorthand for the phenomenon of conversion. But we have to be careful when we speak of Saul's experience as a "conversion," because he did *not* change from one religion to another. That's not the way he perceived the event, and that's not the way he spoke of it.

Saul was a zealous Jew traveling to Damascus to stamp out the early Christian movement among Jews. At the time, there was no such thing as "Christianity" or a "Church" that existed apart from the synagogue. Followers of Jesus worshiped with ordinary Jews, in their ordinary places of worship. In fact, Paul himself would, all his life, continue to identify himself as a Jew (Acts 21:39).

Saul saw his conversion not as a renunciation of the religion of his childhood and youth, but rather its fulfillment. He spoke of it in terms of a vocation, like the call received by the prophets of the Old Testament (see 1 Sam 3:4). He spoke of it in terms of an apparition, a revelation, and a commissioning (see Gal 1:15-16; 1 Cor 15:8-10), but never as an abandonment of the religion of Israel.

Saul learned that the day he had longed for — the day of salvation, the day of the Messiah — had arrived. He had indeed undergone a conversion, but it was not to a new religion. It was, instead, a deeper experience, a new vision of the religion he had always known and loved. Before that blinding flash of light, he had known Jesus only "according to the flesh" (2 Cor 5:16). But he came to understand that, in the encounter on the Damascus road, God "was pleased to reveal his Son to me" (Gal 1:16).

Saul "went away into Arabia" (Gal 1:17) for three years, perhaps to pray and meditate upon the Scriptures and the recent turn of events, perhaps to receive further training from the followers of Jesus.

Eventually, though, he returned to Damascus and entered the synagogues he had once intended to purge, and there he preached Jesus as "the Son of God," shocking and infuriating his fellow Jews. They plotted to kill him for his traitorous reversal, and so he fled to Jerusalem, where the drama replayed itself: Saul preached Jesus as the Messiah, and soon he was the object of a murder plot.

Those who followed "the Way" sought to protect him by sending him off to his home city of Tarsus (Acts 9:20-30).

First Missionary Journey

Some time later, Saul was selected to join a missionary team led by the Apostle Barnabas (Acts 13). Setting out from Seleucia, the seaport of Syrian Antioch, they sailed some 80 miles to the island of Cyprus. There they preached in the synagogues, where the Roman proconsul was converted (Acts 13:6-12).

During the course of the trip, Saul gradually came to the forefront, emerging as the leader of the team of evangelists. Now in the

Gentile world, he used his Roman name, Paul, almost exclusively.

The journey drew them northward into Perga in Pamphylia (lands now in Turkey). They continued inland to Pisidian Antioch, where Paul, invited by the leaders of the synagogue, preached his first recorded sermon (Acts 13:16-51). The Apostles enjoyed great success among both Jews and Gentiles, but their Jewish opponents plotted against them and "stirred up persecution."

Paul and Barnabas left for Iconium (Acts 14) and enjoyed similar success there, until "unbelieving Jews stirred up the Gentiles and poisoned their minds" against them. They toughed it out, until a mob made ready to stone them. Then they fled from there to Lystra, where again they preached the Gospel. The people were so impressed by Paul and Barnabas that they tried to worship them as gods. But the mob was easily swayed. Soon, the persecutors from Antioch and Iconium, still in pursuit, incited the people of Lystra to stone Paul, expel him, and leave him for dead.

He did not die, however, and went on with Barnabas to preach in Derbe before returning to all the previous stops on their route, appointing elders (clergy) for each of the churches before sailing home to Antioch. At Antioch, Paul drew a lesson from his hardships — "through many tribulations we must enter the kingdom of God" (Acts 14:22) — and he explained to the believers "how he had opened a door of faith to the Gentiles" (Acts 14:27). This was for Paul the fulfillment of God's plan for Israel through the kingdom of David. "And the kingdom / . . . shall be given to the people of the saints of the Most High; / their kingdom shall be an everlasting kingdom, and all dominions shall serve and obey them" (Dan 7:27).

The Council of Jerusalem

But not everyone was pleased by St. Paul's announcement. In fact, a group from Judea went to Antioch to inform Gentile converts that, in order to become Christians, they first must keep the Jewish ritual and dietary laws.

Their terms were stark: "Unless you are circumcised according to the custom of Moses, you cannot be saved" (Acts 15:1). Paul and Barnabas took issue with this, and went with a delegation to Jerusalem to refer the question to the Apostles.

The delegation reported on the success of their missionary journey, news that was welcomed warmly by the Apostles. Some Pharisees, however, continued in opposition. They wished to reserve salvation as a separatist, nationalist movement. They wanted Gentiles to become Jews and observe all the laws and customs of Judaism; thus, this faction became known as "Judaizers."

In Jerusalem, the Apostles gathered to hear both sides of the debate. Peter settled the matter by announcing that Jews and Gentiles alike were saved by faith and not by adherence to Jewish ritual law. James followed by putting forth a sensitive pastoral plan for integrating communities of Gentiles and Jews — requiring upright moral behavior and the avoidance of pagan idolatrous practices. The Apostles sent Paul and Barnabas back to Antioch to make the announcement.

Still, the Judaizers did not relent, and even Peter seemed intimidated by them. Paul, in his Letter to the Galatians, tells how Peter was later reluctant to share a meal with Gentile Christians in Antioch. Paul recalls that he "opposed [Peter] to his face," saying, "If you, though a Jew, live like a Gentile and not like a Jew, how can you compel the Gentiles to live like Jews?" (Gal 2:11, 14). Some readers have wrongly interpreted this as Paul's rejection of Peter's supreme authority among the Apostles. But it is exactly the opposite. Paul did not oppose Peter's doctrine, but rather his cowardice and insincerity (Gal 2:13). He urged the first pope to live up to his own infallible teaching.

Second Missionary Journey

St. Paul made his second missionary journey accompanied by Silas (Acts 15-18). They traveled a land route this time (Acts 16), through Syria and Paul's native Cilicia, revisiting

Derbe and Lystra before heading north to Galatia, where Paul stayed for an extended time (Gal 4:13-14). According to Acts, "the Spirit of Jesus" prevented Paul from entering Bithynia and impelled him westward, toward Greece and into Europe. This direction was confirmed in a vision.

So he crossed the straits and went on to Europe (Acts 16-17), and with him went the Gospel. In Greece, Paul and Silas saw great success — along with the usual adversities, mobs, and brief imprisonments — as they established churches in Philippi, Thessalonika, and Beroea. Paul went on to Athens, where he preached before the intellectual elites of the city, drawing from his deep knowledge of Greek culture, literature, and religion. But he converted only a few.

Paul traveled on to Corinth, a center of government and trade in the region (Acts 18). There he worked with a welcoming populace, both Jews and Gentiles, and he stayed for a year and a half. It was from Corinth that he wrote the first two of his letters, to the Thessalonians.

After almost three years of travel, he wished to be back in Jerusalem for the feast of Pentecost, so he returned eastward by sea to Caesarea (making stops along the way), and from Caesarea he went to Jerusalem.

Third Missionary Journey
On his third missionary journey (Acts 18-21), St. Paul went by land to Galatia, returning to his old home in Tarsus. He set up shop at Ephesus, where he stayed almost three years (Acts 19), preaching, working miracles, and converting many people. He ran afoul of the silversmiths, who manufactured idols for the great temple of the goddess Diana, because they saw the Gospel as a threat to their livelihood. In Ephesus, Paul wrote his First Letter to the Corinthians.

Paul stopped in Macedonia on his way to Greece (Acts 20). On returning to his home base, he kept the Feast of Unleavened Bread in Philippi. He made many more stops on his way to Cyprus, and then sailed to Syria. He went by land to Jerusalem.

Imprisonments and Martyrdom

Arriving in Jerusalem after his third missionary journey, St. Paul told St. James and the elders about his successes among the Gentiles (Acts 21). They rejoiced. But then the specter of the Judaizers returned, as the elders told Paul of rumors that he had been teaching Jews to abandon the Law of Moses. To quell his opponents, the elders asked Paul to make a vow of purification according to ritual law, and Paul complied.

Some Jews, however, spread a false rumor that Paul had brought a Gentile into the Temple — a capital crime. The mob was ready to kill Paul when Roman soldiers arrived to restore order. The Romans arrested him. But Paul's opponents gave conflicting accounts of his offenses, so the Roman tribune had him locked up for interrogation. Reassuring the man that he was not a rebel, Paul gained permission to address the crowd (Acts 22). He told the mob his conversion story, which was met with jeers. Afterward, the tribune learned that Paul was a Roman citizen and so was obliged to give him a higher standard of treatment under imperial law.

The tribune summoned the council of the Jews, and Paul appealed to the Pharisees among them against the Sadducees, who held power (Acts 23). This threw the assembly into violent disarray. The tribune had Paul returned to jail for the Apostle's own protection. After surviving an assassination attempt, Paul was brought before Felix the governor. Members of the council accused Paul again of rabble-rousing and blasphemy.

Paul was kept in detention for two years, even as Felix ended his term and was succeeded by a new governor, Festus (Acts 25). Brought before Festus, Paul exercised his right as a citizen and appealed for a trial before Caesar. Festus, then, was required to send Paul on to Rome. It was a strategic move, either on Paul's part or on the part of the Holy Spirit. Now, at last, he would go to Rome, "the capital of the world," to preach the Gospel.

He was sent by sea, but his vessel was shipwrecked near the island of Malta (Acts 27-28).

Paul seized the opportunity to evangelize the natives, who eagerly received the Gospel. Paul spent two years in Rome under house arrest, but was given much freedom to continue his work. In his Letter to the Philippians, he mentions some passing details of his circumstances in Rome (1:13; 4:22).

We see little more of Paul in the Scriptures. It seems likely that his appeal to Caesar worked in his favor, and he was released. In his Letter to the Romans (15:24), he had expressed a desire to go to Spain, and local traditions indicate that he achieved that goal. The ancients are unanimous in testifying that Paul died a martyr's death in the great persecution under Emperor Nero, between A.D. 64 and 67. It is said that Peter and Paul were martyred in Rome on the same day, June 29: Peter by crucifixion and Paul by beheading, since Roman citizens were spared the indignity of the cross. Paul's relics are housed in Rome beneath the altar of the great basilica church that bears his name: St. Paul Outside-the-Walls.

3. St. Paul's Thought

Why a Pharisee? Why Saul?
Why did God call Saul to be an Apostle?
Unlike the other Apostles, St. Paul wasn't
summoned during Jesus' earthly ministry.
Saul's vocation came while he was on his way
to persecute the Church. Why?

The original Apostles were sent first to the
lands of historic Israel (see Acts 1:8). Their
mission was to convince the Chosen People
that they had missed the long-awaited Messiah — that Jesus had, in fact, been misjudged
by the priests, theologians, and those who
were most knowledgeable in the Law. Could
the original Apostles — laborers and
unlearned men — have presented a credible
witness against such experts?

It was a struggle against the odds — until
God called forth a brilliant student of
Jerusalem's most respected teacher. Up to that
point, common tradesmen had been pitted

against scholars. Now the debate was, even by worldly standards, more equally matched.

But why, then, did God send Saul off to the Gentiles? Again, only a rabbi of Saul's brilliance could persuade his fellow Pharisees that the ritual laws of the Jews — animal sacrifice, kosher laws, and the calendar — did not apply to Gentiles. The authorities might dismiss, unheard, the arguments of Galilean fishermen. But they couldn't ignore Saul, the student of Gamaliel.

For Jews, the most offensive feature of the Gospel was that Gentiles were now to be accepted as equal members of God's family. How could first-century Jews assimilate that truth by natural means after centuries of seeing foreigners as untouchables? History required a man of Saul's learning and prestige to make the argument with subtlety and precision. This explains his success, but it also explains the difficulty that many Gentiles have in following Paul's arguments. Most of us are not as thoroughly trained in the Scriptures as the ancient Pharisees were.

The Word of the Cross

Another difficulty for Saul the Pharisee was the cross. "Christ crucified," he later explained, was "a stumbling block to Jews" (1 Cor 1:23; see also Gal 5:11). Crucifixion was the most humiliating and degrading method of torture and execution. The Law of Moses cursed anyone who was hanged on a tree (Deut 21:23; Gal 3:13). And a crucified and bloody corpse was not any Pharisee's image of the promised Messiah. But it was, by their measure, the just punishment due to a man who called himself the Son of God. "This was why the Jews sought all the more to kill him, because he not only broke the Sabbath but also called God his Father, making himself equal with God" (Jn 5:18).

The breakthrough for Saul came when he encountered Jesus and discovered that Jesus was indeed who he claimed to be. When Saul saw the light and heard the voice, he knew that he was in God's presence, and so he used a divine form of address: "Who are you, Lord?" And the voice responded, "I am Jesus"

(Acts 9:5). Thus, Saul realized instantly that Jesus was alive and that he was divine. God "was pleased to reveal his Son to me," he later said (Gal 1:16).

As the Son of God, Jesus was indeed worthy of worship — and his cross was not divinely cursed, but a revelation of divine self-giving:

> *Christ Jesus, ... though he was in the form of God, did not count equality with God a thing to be grasped, but emptied himself, taking the form of a servant, being born in the likeness of men. And being found in human form he humbled himself and became obedient unto death, even death on a cross.* (Phil 2:5-8)

Jesus' life and death became, for St. Paul, a revelation of God's love in action. Calvary reveals the truth of what it means to be God.

The Good News of Salvation
Saul had expected the Messiah to be a king who would restore the house of David. God sent his own eternal Son, incarnate as a Son of

David. Saul had expected deliverance to bring peace, prosperity, and freedom to obey the Law of Moses. But God's idea of salvation was far greater: he would deliver his people from sin; he would deliver them from death; and greatest of all, he would deliver them to share his own life.

Salvation was not merely *from* something; it was *for* something. God delivered his people *from* sin so that they might become his sons and daughters. Furthermore, God extended that salvation beyond the bounds of Israel to encompass all the peoples of the world, thus fulfilling his promise to Abraham that "all the nations of the earth shall bless themselves by him" (Gen 18:18).

Saul of Tarsus became St. Paul the Apostle in order to spread that Good News. "The Gentiles are fellow heirs, members of the same body, and partakers of the promise in Christ Jesus.... Of this gospel I was made a minister ... to preach to the Gentiles the unsearchable riches of Christ" (Eph 3:6, 7, 8). And Paul was such a great Apostle for the same reason that Saul was such a great persecutor. All it took was an encounter with Christ to redirect his zeal.

Salvation and Sonship

Our adoption as God's children is the deepest meaning of salvation. It encompasses redemption, justification, and all the other metaphors: "But when the goodness and loving kindness of God our Savior appeared, he saved us, not because of deeds done by us in righteousness, but in virtue of his own mercy, by the washing of regeneration and renewal in the Holy Spirit, which he poured out upon us richly through Jesus Christ our Savior, so that we might be justified by his grace and become heirs in hope of eternal life" (Titus 3:4-7).

When St. Paul spoke of deliverance, it was almost as if human language was inadequate to express what Jesus Christ had accomplished. He exhausted one metaphor after another. The Apostle used the terminology of the courtroom, saying that we have been justified — that is, acquitted in a court of law (see Rom 5:16-17). He drew analogies from the marketplace, to make the point that we have been "redeemed": "You were bought with a price" (1 Cor 7:23; see also 2 Titus 2:13-14). He drew military analogies, portraying us as the object of a divine rescue mission (2 Tim 4:18). He said we were "set free" from "slavery" (Gal 5:1).

But all the metaphors seem to lead to one that is his favorite: our adoption as children of God. It would have been a grand thing if God had just delivered Israel from oppression. It would have been greater still if God had forgiven all the sins of a fallen world. But he did so much more in Jesus Christ. He brought about "redemption" for the sake of "adoption" and "inheritance" (Rom 8:15-23) — "to redeem those who were under the law, so that we might receive adoption as sons" (Gal 4:5).

The Importance of Covenant

Some non-Catholic interpreters would have us stop short of this reality. They put the focus instead on justification — and they interpret "justice" by the standards of the modern courtroom. But in doing so, they are ignoring the cultural and religious context of St. Paul's many metaphors. Supremely important for him (as for all first-century Jews) was the idea of covenant. It was the covenant with God that constituted Israel as God's Chosen People. Covenant was the context for all of Israel's life and Law.

Covenant created a family bond — and with Jesus' "new covenant" (1 Cor 11:25), that family bond was made immeasurably stronger. Salvation has made us like Jesus — children of God in the eternal Son of God (see Gal 3:26) — "partakers of the divine nature" (2 Pet 1:4). By means of Jesus' New Covenant, we enter God's immediate family. Fidelity to the covenant is what Paul intends when he uses terms like *justice* and *justification*. Justice is not merely God's rewarding the good and punishing the bad, but rather God's fidelity to his covenant, in spite of mankind's repeated infidelities. "Let God be true though every man be false" (Rom 3:4). In Christ, God kept his covenant promises to Abraham and David.

Paul knew that God was not content to be merely our judge. He wished to be our Father (see Eph 1:5). And that is the very essence of salvation in Christ.

This was God's saving plan since "before the foundation of the world" (Eph 1:4). In the covenant with Abraham, God had promised blessings to the patriarch's offspring (Gal 3:16), foretelling that "all the nations of the earth shall bless themselves by him" (Gen 18:18). Jesus is Abraham's offspring (Gal 3:16) — and all believers share the blessings of the covenant, precisely because he has borne the covenant curses due to sins of mankind (Gal 3:13). Thus, the blessings now belong to all those who live "in Christ," those whom God "destined . . . in love to be his sons through Jesus Christ" (Eph 1:5) — destined long before Abraham, long before Adam, in fact from all eternity.

The Scandal of God's Fatherhood

At the heart of St. Paul's gospel, then, was the revelation of God's fatherhood. In Paul's world, that was a shocking claim.

It was customary for Jews to call upon God as "Father" of their nation (see Jn 8:41), but *not* as Father to an individual. To make such a claim, they rightly assumed, was in some way to make oneself "equal with God" — for earthly children do share a common nature with their fathers. This is true of both natural and adoptive relations. Human adults can adopt or conceive only human children. No matter how much I love my pets, I can't adopt them as family members.

The shocking truth is that Jesus *does* share God's nature. Even more shocking is that Jesus also wants us to share the divine nature of his heavenly Father. That was, and is, a religious bombshell.

It's one thing to say that God is metaphorically "father" to a nation or to the world, because he created both out of nothing. But it's quite another to say that God is eternally "Father" by nature, and that all earthly fatherhood reflects that eternal truth (Eph 3:14). If God is eternally Father, then there must be an eternal "Child." To the mind of a Pharisee —

a mind trained in monotheism — that seemed to imply a threat to God's oneness and transcendence. We can only imagine the blinding force of the event when God "was pleased to reveal his Son" (Gal 1:16) to Paul.

It's important that we get this right. Paul was not saying that God is somehow *like* a Father. No, he meant that God is *eternally* Father because the Word is his eternal Son (see Phil 2:6; Gal 4:4; 2 Cor 8:9; Col 1:15-19).

We Are "In Christ"

What's more, St. Paul wants us to know that we, through baptism, have come to share in Christ's sonship:

> *He saved us, not because of deeds done by us in righteousness, but in virtue of his own mercy, by the washing of regeneration and renewal in the Holy Spirit, which he poured out upon us richly through Jesus Christ our Savior, so that we might be justified by his grace and become heirs in hope of eternal life.* (Titus 3:5-7; see also Gal 3:26-27)

Paul speaks repeatedly of us as living "in Christ" (see Rom 8:1). Most famously, he quotes a pagan poet to make his point: "In [God] we live and move and have our being... 'For we are indeed his offspring'" (Acts 17:28). He also speaks of Christ as living in us (Gal 2:20).

We are sons and daughters in the eternal Son of God. Though Christ had the "form of God" (Phil 2:6), he poured himself out to take on a human "form" (Phil 2:7). Why did he do that? So that we might be in him and he in us. God "destined us in love to be his sons through Jesus Christ, according to the purpose of his will" (Eph 1:5). "For in Christ Jesus you are all sons of God, through faith" (Gal 3:26).

The Jews of Paul's time often spoke of the fellowship they shared with one another because of the covenant. The Hebrew word for this bond is *chaburah*; it is usually rendered in Greek as *koinonia*. But the Jews never applied those words to the relationship between humans and God. Not until Paul, that is.

The Apostle made clear that Jesus' salvation had shattered not only the boundaries between Israel and the nations, but also between God and the world. Now God could share fellowship and communion with all his people in the Church: "The cup of blessing which we bless, is it not a participation [*koinonia*] in the blood of Christ? The bread which we break, is it not a participation [*koinonia*] in the body of Christ?" (1 Cor 10:16). Our life in Christ is our share, our participation, our communion in God's life. It is, at last, *chaburah* between God and the human race.

So close is our familial bond with God that — in the "Spirit of sonship" — we, like Jesus, may address God as *Abba* (Rom 8:15; Gal 4:6), the intimate name that Hebrew-speaking children use to address their "Papa."

The Church at the Center

Believers share in the body of Christ, and the Church becomes the body of Christ. That truth impressed itself upon Saul at the very moment of his conversion. He heard the voice of Jesus say, "'Saul, Saul, why do you persecute *me*?... 'I am Jesus, whom you are persecuting'" (Acts 9:4-5, emphasis added). Christ could have said, "Why are you persecuting my Church?" or "my people?" But he didn't. Instead, he identified himself with his followers: whatsoever Saul did to them, he did to Jesus.

St. Paul begins to work this out in his First Letter to the Corinthians, where the resurrected body of Christ turns out to be a Eucharistic mystery: "The bread which we break, is it not a participation in the body of Christ? Because there is one bread, we who are many are one body, for we all partake of the one bread" (10:16-17). In the following chapter, he makes clear that the Eucharistic species contain Christ really present (see 11:24-29), a "body" that must be discerned by faith. But he is equally clear that this Eucharistic body transforms believers into a mystical body — the Church as the body of Christ on earth.

Paul returns to this theme throughout his letters. "The Church ... is [Christ's] body, the fulness of him who fills all in all" (Eph 1:22-23).

"Now you are the body of Christ and individually members of it" (1 Cor 12:27). "Christ is the head of the Church, his body, and . . . we are members of his body" (Eph 5:23, 30; see also Col 1:18). Again, it is the Eucharist that unites the "members" with their "head."

Through our integrated life in the Church, we are "building up the body of Christ" (Eph 4:11-12). Like the organs and limbs in a human body, we all have parts to play in the Church:

> *For just as the body is one and has many members, and all the members of the body, though many, are one body, so it is with Christ. For by one Spirit we were all baptized into one body — Jews or Greeks, slaves or free — and all were made to drink of one Spirit.*
>
> *For the body does not consist of one member but of many.* (1 Cor 12:12-14)

Paul speaks of our incorporation by baptism in starkly realistic terms. It is not merely a psychological phenomenon. It's not just an "attitude adjustment." It's not merely a metaphor or a moral quality. Our union with Christ is profound and transforming. Christ gives us the grace to live a holy life — to live life with *his own* holiness, in his body. The holiness he gives us is essentially connected to our Eucharistic worship. It is our sacramental share in God's life, his nature.

The sacraments are the source of our power to live moral lives. Because of the sacraments, we live our lives *in Christ, by his grace, sharing in his righteousness.* Thus, Paul speaks of us as a "new creation" (2 Cor 5:17; Gal 6:15) in baptism. And he is not referring to our transformation after death, in heaven. He speaks in the present tense when he says: "And we all, with unveiled face, beholding the glory of the Lord, are being changed into his likeness from one degree of glory to another" (2 Cor 3:18). "Though our outer [nature] is wasting away, our inner [nature] is being renewed every day" (2 Cor 4:16). We live "in the Spirit," and "the life of Jesus may be manifested" even now "in our mortal flesh" (2 Cor 4:11).

Paul sees the sacraments in realist, participationist, and mystical terms. God himself, says the Apostle, will "provide the way of escape" for us, beyond sin, beyond death (1 Cor 10:13) — and that way of escape is the Eucharist, as he shows us in the subsequent verses in 1 Corinthians (10:14-17). The Eucharist gives us the power to live as Christ in his body.

Faith and Works

Thus, it would be a mistake to believe that our moral actions are irrelevant to our salvation. St. Paul makes clear that we are called not merely to faith, but to the "*obedience* of faith" (Rom 1:5, 16:26). He says that it is "not the hearers of the law who are righteous before God, but the doers of the law who will be justified" (Rom 2:13). What God wants from us is "faith working through love" (Gal 5:6). Or, as Paul's fellow Apostle St. James puts it: "A man is justified by works and not by faith alone" (Jas 2:24), for "faith by itself, if it has no works, is dead" (Jas 2:17).

Paul indeed asserts that "a man is justified by faith apart from works of law" (Rom 3:28). But by "works of law" he does not mean the moral law, and certainly not the Ten Commandments. He is not exempting us from good behavior or giving us a pass on our sins. In the first century, "works of law" was a stock phrase for the ceremonial requirements: animal sacrifice, circumcision, and the cultic calendar. In the New Covenant, we are not required to observe these, as the Jews did in the Old Covenant.

It's not that Paul is opposed in principle to ritual worship. He maintains, for example, that baptism is powerful in a way that circumcision was not. Baptism causes our death to sin and our union with Christ. The New Covenant sacraments, compared to the Old, are fewer, easier to perform, and far more powerful.

The sacraments give us the power we need to live in righteousness. St. Augustine put it memorably: *The law was given so grace we'd seek; grace was given so the law we can keep.* Nevertheless, we remain free to separate ourselves from the sacraments — and from Christ — through grave sin. Paul never preaches absolute eternal security. He does ask, "Who shall separate us from the love of Christ?" (Rom 8:35). But we need to continue reading past that question mark. Paul goes on to ask in the same verse, "Shall tribulation, or distress, or persecution, or famine, or nakedness, or peril, or sword?" He speaks of our perseverance through suffering, not sin! He does not ask if murder, theft, lying, or adultery "shall separate us from Christ's love," because he knows that we are free to separate ourselves by such grave transgressions against God's moral law.

While suffering unites us with Christ's suffering on the cross, sin can certainly separate us from him. We have the Spirit so that we may keep the Law. God gives us that freedom, and with it comes the freedom to reject him as well.

The Problem of Pain
In identifying believers with Christ, St. Paul has given us the key to understanding the

mystery of suffering: "I consider that the sufferings of this present time are not worth com-
paring with the glory that is to be revealed to
us" (Rom 8:18).

Though he trained his sights on glory, Paul
knew that he would have to suffer much while
he was "in the flesh" (Gal 2:20), and that one
day he would die (Phil 1:23).

For those of us who do not share Paul's
great theological gifts, suffering and death
remain profound mysteries. We know that
they entered the world because of sin (Rom
5:12). Yet we also believe that Christ has set us
free from the power of sin and death (Rom
8:2). If that is so, why must we still suffer and
die?

Paul taught that Jesus Christ himself suffered, not as a *substitute* for sinful humanity,
but as our *representative*. Thus, Christ's saving
passion didn't exempt us from suffering, but
instead endowed our suffering with divine
power and redemptive value.

Paul could even "rejoice" in his troubles,
"knowing that suffering produces endurance,

and endurance produces character, and character produces hope, and hope does not disappoint us, because God's love has been poured into our hearts through the Holy Spirit" (Rom 5:3-5).

Through the Spirit of God, we are children of God. And God gives his children everything he has, sharing even his divine nature. But he did not spare his Son from suffering. Suffering was central to Jesus' mission as redeemer. And so it is part of our share in his life and mission.

Thus, suffering is not an optional component of Christian life. Paul tells us that "we are children of God ... fellow heirs with Christ, provided we suffer with him in order that we may also be glorified with him" (Rom 8:16, 17).

So: No suffering, no glory.

And yet it is not the magnitude of Christ's suffering that saves us, but rather the magnitude of his love. Love turns his suffering into sacrifice. And that love is the Eucharist. It is the Eucharist that turns Calvary into a sacrifice rather than merely an execution. Paul knows that suffering without love is unendurable, but also that love without suffering is impossible.

We share in Christ's love through the Eucharist; and so our suffering — like Jesus' suffering — has redemptive power. "Now I rejoice in my sufferings for your sake, and in my flesh I complete what is lacking in Christ's afflictions for the sake of his body, that is, the Church" (Col 1:24). Redemptive suffering is a participation in the life of Christ, in the body of Christ, in the Eucharist, and in the Church. Through the Spirit, we have communion with him, and in our bodies we reproduce and re-present his life and love, his sonship and sacrifice, his death and resurrection.

And that in itself is a privilege and a source of peace: "For as we share abundantly in Christ's sufferings, so through Christ we share abundantly in comfort too" (2 Cor 1:5).

Glory in the Cross

We share in Christ's life, and so we share in his cross. It is by way of the cross that we come to share in his glory. St. Paul mapped out our way in the great hymn to Christ at the heart of his Letter to the Philippians. It bears repeating here:

> *Have this mind among yourselves, which was in Christ Jesus, who, though he was in the form of God, did not count equality with God a thing to be grasped, but emptied himself, taking the form of a servant, being born in the likeness of men. And being found in human form he humbled himself and became obedient unto death, even death on a cross. Therefore God has highly exalted him and bestowed on him the name which is above every name, that at the name of Jesus every knee should bow, in heaven and on earth and under the earth, and every tongue confess that Jesus Christ is Lord, to the glory of God the Father.* (Phil 2:5-11)

If we are to be like Christ, the way is clear: we must not grasp at our privileges, but rather empty ourselves, as Jesus did. Christ gave everything he had, for our sakes. He gave as God gave, holding nothing back. He gave his body to us in the Eucharist. He gave his life for us on the cross.

For us, sharing the life of the Son of God means living as he lived, giving as he gave, giving our lives, moment by moment, for the sake of others. "Present your bodies," Paul tells us, "as a living sacrifice, holy and acceptable to God, which is your spiritual worship" (Rom12:1).

We choose to be weak by worldly standards because Christ did. "God chose what is weak in the world to shame the strong" (1 Cor 1:27). For the Lord himself said to Paul, "My grace is sufficient for you, for my power is made perfect in weakness" (2 Cor 12:9).

Thus, the cross becomes the focal point for Paul. For him the cross is "power" (1 Cor 1:17-18) and glory (Gal 6:14) and peace (Eph 2:16).

Paul sees no other reason for "glory except in the cross of our Lord Jesus Christ, by which the world has been crucified to me, and I to the world" (Gal 6:14). It is by the blood of Christ, shed on the cross, that we have become "children of God, and if children, then heirs, heirs of God and fellow heirs with Christ." But his way must become our way, and we know it as the Way of the Cross. We are God's children now, "fellow heirs with Christ, provided we suffer with him in order that we may also be glorified with him" (Rom 8:16-17).

4. St. Paul's Letters

The Question of Authorship

Christian tradition attributes 13 (sometimes 14) letters to the Apostle to the Gentiles. We should not be surprised that these letters vary widely in style and content.

St. Paul's letters, after all, served many different purposes, for many different churches, set in many different cultures and experiencing vastly different needs. They were written over a span of more than a decade — a period when Paul matured both naturally and supernaturally.

His range is remarkable. Romans is a doctrinal *tour de force*. Galatians is a stern rebuke. Philemon is an ingratiating plea. Philippians is full of warm encouragement and joyful gratitude. The letters to Timothy and Titus are handbooks of practical advice, from an experienced pastor to his young colleagues.

This variety of styles and concerns has led some modern scholars to question whether all the "Pauline" letters could have been written by the same author. The answer should be an immediate yes from anyone whose work demands extensive writing over a long period of time. A writer's style, content, and vocabulary can change often depending on his goals, audience, circumstances — and even his mood!

What's more, Paul's letters were, by his own admission, sometimes drafted by an associate or dictated to a secretary. These fellow workers are often identified in the salutation or sign-off of the letters. First Corinthians is addressed from Paul and Sosthenes; First and Second Thessalonians from Paul, Silvanus, and Timothy. Philippians, Colossians, and Philemon come from Paul and Timothy. In Romans, Tertius identifies himself as the *writer* of the epistle (16:22), and Timothy is, again, identified as a co-worker (16:21).

Paul remains, however, the mind and authority behind all the letters — and the

Church's Tradition, witnessed by the Fathers, ascribes the letters' authorship to him. A growing number of scholars have come, by way of research, to similar conclusions.

Why do some scholars question Paul's authorship? Mostly because there are real differences from letter to letter. Can these differences be explained by other factors? I think so. It is worth mentioning that at least some of the more critical attitudes toward Paul have sprung from modern interpreters' anti-institutional bias. Protestant Pauline scholar Michael J. Gorman goes so far as to call it an "anti-Catholic bias," which has allowed "theological preferences" to affect historical judgments. Some scholars, for example, reject the letters to Timothy and Titus simply because they assume the existence of Church hierarchy, liturgy, and a well-developed orthodoxy in doctrinal matters.

For the limited purposes of this little book, we will simply acknowledge that the issue of authorship is certainly complex, and then proceed with our discussion of the letters that appear in the biblical canon under the name of St. Paul. We'll consider the letters in canonical order, since that is how most readers encounter them. We will discuss, separately, the special case of the Letter to the Hebrews.

Romans

This letter was written during the last phase of St. Paul's third missionary journey, probably around A.D. 57-58. Rome, as the capital of a vast empire, was a bustling center of military power, commerce, and culture. Paul wrote to a vibrant and well-established Christian community, whose members he had never met. He wanted to introduce himself and to prepare the Romans for his planned visit. He also hoped to ease tensions between Gentiles and Jews, as each group took pride in its place in the history of salvation. The Jews boasted that they were heirs to the promises; the Gentiles held that they had superseded the Jews as God's people.

Paul makes an argument for the unity and catholicity of the Church. He emphasizes faith and baptism — justification and sonship —

over against works of the old Law, such as circumcision. Composed late in his apostolic
career, Romans reflects Paul's mature theological reflection. He speaks of mankind's need for
salvation since the sin of Adam; of God's
mighty deeds in calling and delivering his people; of the place of Israel and its restoration;
and of the fullness of salvation in Jesus Christ.
Romans has influenced Christian theology and
history more than any other of Paul's letters.

1 Corinthians

St. Paul wrote this letter while he was staying
in Ephesus, probably during his third missionary journey, around A.D. 56. Corinth was a
prosperous commercial and administrative
center, a way station on voyages between Asia
and Italy. It was famous for sporting events and
infamous for its low morals. Paul himself
founded the Church in Corinth (see Acts 18:1-
18) and spent a long time there. Now, after
several years' absence, he has heard reports of
the community's lack of discipline, evident in
sexual immorality, division, liturgical abuses,

neglect of the poor, and disbelief in core doctrines.

Paul writes, like a father to his children, to remedy the situation. He instructs the Corinthians in basic Eucharistic piety, which should be at the heart of their Christian life. He discusses lifelong celibacy as well as Christian marriage. He is especially sensitive to the difficulties of living in a predominantly pagan environment. Idolatry is everywhere, and it even affects the cuts of meat offered in the marketplace. Wealth and sophistication bring their own perils, especially pride and selfishness. Paul urges the Corinthians to turn instead toward the needs of one another and the greater good of the whole "body," the Church. He speaks of the Church as the Temple of the Spirit, where Christ's sacrifice is offered. His exhortation climaxes with the famous hymn to selfless charity: "Love is patient...."

2 Corinthians

This letter was written shortly after 1 Corinthians, as a follow-up, and it is the most personal and autobiographical of St. Paul's writings. The Apostle wrote from Macedonia, probably in A.D. 56. He wrote to counteract the influence of "false apostles" who had tried to undermine his work in Corinth and had even attacked him personally during a recent visit. Most of the Corinthian Christians had failed to rise to his defense. Though some later repented, others did not, and the community remained divided. Chapters 11-12 provide a remarkable catalog of sufferings endured by the Apostle, demonstrating that weakness is his strength (12:10). By writing, Paul hoped to strengthen his loyal base and defend his apostolic authority against his opposition. He also wrote to solicit funds to support the poor Christians in Jerusalem. Second Corinthians may actually be the fusion of two or more of Paul's letters.

Galatians

The Letter to the Galatians was probably written in the early or mid-50s A.D. The Roman province of Galatia covered a large area in what is now central Turkey.

The letter is St. Paul's impassioned defense against Judaizers, who pressured Gentile Christians to be circumcised and to observe the ceremonial laws of the Old Covenant. Paul explains that the New Covenant established by Christ has dispensed with the ritual obligations of the Law of Moses. By dying on the cross, Christ redeemed mankind from the curses of the Old Covenant and released the divine blessings of the New Covenant, inaugurating a new creation and a renewed Israel. Christ's New Covenant fulfills God's covenant with Abraham, which promised blessings for all nations through the family of Abraham; at the same time, it terminated the Mosaic covenant, which was restricted to Israel. Whoever has faith in Christ becomes a spiritual descendant of Abraham and a child of God by adoption.

Paul's tone is sometimes furious, and he resorts even to name-calling in order to make his points, which he considers to be of paramount importance. But the overall thrust of the letter is positive, giving guidance for the true freedom that comes through Christian living.

Ephesians

This letter was written during one of St. Paul's terms of imprisonment, most likely his house arrest in Rome in A.D. 60-62. Thus, it is the first of the so-called "Captivity Letters." (The others are Philippians, Colossians, and Phile-mon.) It is addressed to the Church in the leading metropolis of the Roman province of Asia (now southwest Turkey). Paul spent sev-eral years ministering to the people of Ephesus.

Much of Ephesians concerns itself with theology in the strictest sense: reflection about God and his mysterious saving "plan" for his-tory. Paul explains that God had destined us in love to be his children before the founda-tion of the world. The key to understanding all intervening history is the saving death of Jesus Christ, which was a sacrifice for the redemption of all people, both Israel and the Gentiles. Now enthroned in heaven, Christ rules over heaven and earth, mankind and the angels.

This letter contains Paul's most sustained and developed reflection on the Church, which he sees as the Family of God, the Body of Christ, and the Temple of the Spirit. The vision is international, universal, and truly catholic. To be in the Church, Paul says repeatedly, is to be "in Christ." The Letter to the Ephesians shows Paul's remarkable versatility as he moves from points of mystical theology to nitty-gritty practical advice for married couples.

Philippians

This is another Captivity Letter, and it is addressed to the Church in Philippi, the major city in eastern Macedonia. Philippi was a Roman military colony, mostly Gentile, with only a small Jewish population. St. Paul evangelized the area during his second missionary journey, and he returned there on at least one occasion.

Paul writes to express his gratitude for the Philippians' prayers and financial assistance, which he sees as evidence of their faith. The letter is full of affection and joy, with only a few admonitions regarding threats to the Church's peace: divisions between believers and the possible incursion of Judaizing missionaries.

Philippians is best known for its extended treatment of Jesus as the self-giving servant — the Son of God who set aside his deity to become the humblest of men and to die the most humiliating death. Because of this, God the Father exalted him in glory. Thus, Paul exhorts the Church to worship Jesus as God and to imitate the Lord's self-giving. The letter also preserves Paul's most intimate reflection on his own apostolate to date and his readiness for martyrdom. Paul concludes by offering advice for keeping Christian equanimity in all circumstances, whether poverty or prosperity, freedom or persecution.

Colossians

Yet another of St. Paul's Captivity Letters, Colossians was likely composed in Rome in the early 60s A.D. St. Paul writes, in this letter, to a church he has not founded and has never visited. Mainly a Gentile community, Colossae has been evangelized by one of his disciples, Epaphras. It is from Epaphras that Paul learns of the Colossian Church's trouble with some people spreading false doctrines. (It is unclear whether these troublemakers were pagans, wayward Christians, or Jews.)

Stylistically and thematically, Colossians bears some resemblance to Ephesians. Both letters also contain practical advice for marriage and family life. In Colossians, Paul shows Jesus Christ to reign supreme over the cosmos, preeminent as creator over all creatures. Jesus is divine, and he is victorious over all evil spirits. Paul emphasizes that Christians are not bound by the Law of Moses. Christians are complete in Christ.

1 Thessalonians

This is almost certainly the earliest-written of St. Paul's letters. His report in chapter 3 seems to jibe with chapters 17-18 of Acts, so the letter was probably written in A.D. 50-51 from

Corinth. Thessalonika was the capital of the province of Macedonia (in what is now northern Greece).

Paul's main concern in writing is to encourage the Thessalonians as they face persecution. His doctrinal emphasis is on the final judgment, when Christ will come from heaven to deliver the faithful from "the wrath to come" (1:10). The Apostle has heard that some Thessalonians are anxious because their loved ones have died before the Lord's return. Paul assures them that the dead will be raised as Christ was raised. The end will come suddenly, he says, and surprisingly. He exhorts the Thessalonians to moral and spiritual vigilance.

2 Thessalonians

This letter is a follow-up to 1 Thessalonians. The intervening period seems to have brought no relief from persecution, and the congregation seems just as vexed about end-times questions. In fact, the problem has been made worse by a letter, forged in St. Paul's name, that declares that the last days have already arrived and that Jesus' return is imminent. As a result, some people have stopped working. Paul instructs the Thessalonians about the events that will precede Jesus' return, events that have not yet come to pass. Paul admonishes Christians to work diligently, as he himself worked diligently when he was in Thessalonika.

1 Timothy

This letter is the first of the "Pastoral Epistles" attributed to St. Paul. These letters are like handbooks of advice, addressed from one Christian clergyman to another. They focus on pastoral concerns and matters of Church order: liturgy, hierarchy, discipline, catechesis, and sacred Tradition.

Timothy is Paul's longtime companion in mission. Now he is stationed in Ephesus on a special assignment, to counteract the false doctrine ("myths and endless genealogies") spread by some self-appointed teachers whom Paul excommunicated earlier.

Paul's advice is very practical, and it ranges from the qualifications for Church office to the management of charitable works and the establishment of a dress code for worship. Paul addresses the needs of all three orders of clergy: bishops, presbyters (priests), and deacons. The letter seems to have been written from Rome, some time between Paul's first imprisonment there (A.D. 60-62) and the end of his life (A.D. 64 or 67). This letter and the other Pastoral Epistles were revered by the earliest Church Fathers, including St. Clement of Rome, who, according to tradition, was himself a disciple of St. Paul.

2 Timothy

With this letter, St. Paul, abandoned in Rome, probably during Nero's persecution, seeks to summon his loyal companion Timothy, who was still in Ephesus (see 1 Tim above). Paul writes with a strong sense of spiritual fatherhood (2:1). The situation in Ephesus has grown worse, so he urges Timothy to overcome his limitations — youth and timidity — and be strong in God's grace.

As in his previous letter, Paul is especially concerned about speculative doctrines that have been spreading confusion among the Ephesian Christians. He also counsels Timothy on pastoral care amid persecution and internal dissensions. There is an unmistakable valedictory quality to the letter: the elderly Paul seems to be preparing his farewell, but ensuring that his young disciple is ready to bear the faith to the next generation.

Titus

This letter, like the two epistles to Timothy, is a letter of counsel and encouragement addressed to one of St. Paul's former traveling companions, now serving as pastor on the island of Crete. It is imperative for Titus to ordain effective and worthy men as clergy, so Paul sketches the qualities of such a leader. He also emphasizes strong moral behavior — "deeds done by us in righteousness... good deeds" (3:5, 8), even if the moral tone in Crete is very low (1:12) and the local teachers unreliable and divisive (3:9-10).

Philemon
This letter is a plea for clemency on behalf of a runaway slave, Onesimus, who is returning to his master, the Christian to whom the letter is addressed. St. Paul asks that Philemon accept Onesimus back as a brother in Christ rather than as a servant. While the letter is very brief, it makes an eloquent case for the equality of all Christians as members of God's household. Paul refers to his imprisonment, but gives no further details. The letter may have been composed during his detention in Rome in A.D. 60-62.

Hebrews
The Letter to the Hebrews is a special case. Even in ancient times, some Church Fathers questioned whether this letter was the work of St. Paul or rather one of his followers. The text itself does not claim Paul as author, and the letter differs from the others in style and

vocabulary. Still, Hebrews certainly bears the stamp of Paul's influence.

Its central argument is for the superiority of Christ as High Priest of the New Covenant and his sacrifice, over against the animal sacrifices of the Old Covenant. It is possible, some say, that the letter was drafted by an associate who was trained in rhetoric (some see affinities with the language of St. Luke). A small but growing number of modern interpreters have come to attribute the letter's origin to Paul — including respected specialists such as Father James Swetnam, S.J., of the Pontifical Biblical Institute.

5. St. Paul and Us

Many Catholics are skittish about reading St. Paul. It was his texts, after all, that were most invoked by Martin Luther and John Calvin during the controversies of the 16th century. And later anti-Catholic propaganda has also drawn heavily from the Apostle. As the theologian Frank Sheed once said: "A man can never feel quite the same about even the nicest book if he has just been beaten round the head with it."

Yet here we go, paying St. Paul an honor that was condemned by the Protestant reformers: the veneration of the saints.

I'm reminded of the story of John England, the early-19th-century bishop of Charleston, South Carolina. Once, while riding in a stagecoach, he was accosted by a young Protestant preacher. Bishop England recalled: "It was nothing but Paul here, and Paul there, and how could the 'Romanists' answer Paul?"

The bishop winced at the upstart's casual interpretations and familiar terms, till finally he interrupted: "Young man! If you have not faith and piety sufficient to induce you to call the apostle 'Saint Paul,' at least have the good manners to call him 'Mister Paul.'"

St. Paul deserves respect, and he himself would admit as much. Yes, he called himself "the least of the apostles" (1 Cor 15:9) and "the very least of all the saints" (Eph 3:8). But even these self-deprecating titles imply a special dignity and great authority. He may have been the least of saints, but he was still a saint. He may have been the least of the Apostles, but that was itself an extremely elite group. As an Apostle, he spoke with "the Spirit of God" (1 Cor 7:40) and "the mind of Christ" (1 Cor 2:16). He acknowledged an "authority" of which he could legitimately "boast" (2 Cor 10:8), for he was "not at all inferior to these superlative apostles" (2 Cor 12:11). His position merited him a "rightful claim" to respect (1 Cor 9:1-12). He held the power to "pronounce judgment" on sinners (1 Cor 5:3).

By grace, St. Paul bore a dignity that Christians were duty-bound to observe. They looked to him as to a father in the family: "For though you have countless guides in Christ, you do not have many fathers. For I became your father in Christ Jesus through the gospel" (1 Cor 4:15; see also 1 Thess 2:11; Phil 2:22; Philem 10). The Fourth Commandment obliges us to "honor" our fathers, and that means give them our love, respect, obedience, and, of course, imitation. An attentive reading of the letters of St. Paul shows us that he expected no less from us than this basic Christian duty.

Though he knew himself to be "the foremost of sinners" (1 Tim 1:15), St. Paul knew also that he must serve as a model for Christians. "Be imitators of me," he said, "as I am of Christ" (1 Cor 11:1).

St. Paul's favorite term for Christians was "saints" (see, for example, Col 1:2-4). Holiness is our calling and our dignity. Yet he also distinguished between the saints on earth (Col 1:2) and the "saints in light" (Col 1:12) —

what Catholic devotion would later call, respectively, the "Church militant" and the "Church triumphant." The Letter to the Hebrews tells us that the latter are "a cloud of witnesses" (Heb 12:1) around the former.

To the saints on earth who share our calling, we give our love. To the saints in light who have fought the good fight and won the race, we give a special honor called *veneration*. It's not the same kind of honor we give to God alone. It is more like the profound respect we owe our parents and grandparents. We love them so much that we frame their photos and give them a prominent place in our homes. We shouldn't hesitate to ask our parents for prayer, nor should we hesitate to ask our ancestors in the faith — especially someone who has the authority of an Apostle, not to mention the Spirit of God and the mind of Christ!

St. Paul told the Colossians that "we have not ceased to pray for you" (Col 1:9). I believe that this long-ago pledge still holds true. And so we should ask St. Paul's intercession, even as he begged the intercession of other Christians (see Col 4:3).

We need to read St. Paul. We must imitate him as well. But we should also venerate him. To venerate him is to glorify Christ for the grace made manifest in the Apostle's life.

St. Paul himself said it well: "It is no longer I who live, but Christ who lives in me" (Gal 2:20).

6. Quick Reference for Catholic Doctrines and Practices in St. Paul's Life and Work

Baptismal Regeneration: Titus 3:5

Bishops: 1 Timothy 3:1-7; Titus 1:7-9

Celibacy and Chastity: 1 Corinthians 7; 1 Timothy 5:11-12

Confirmation, Sacramental: 2 Corinthians 1:22; Ephesians 1:13

Councils, Authority of: Acts 15

Divinity of Christ: Philippians 2:5-11; Colossians 1:15-16; 2:9; Romans 9:5; Titus 2:13

Eucharist (Real Presence): 1 Corinthians 10:16-17; 11:23-29

Excommunication: 1 Corinthians 5:3-13; 1 Timothy 1:20; Titus 3:10

Forfeiting Salvation: Galatians 5:4; 1 Corinthians 15:1-2

Good Works, Merit of: 1 Corinthians 3:8; 13:2; Galatians 5:6; 2 Timothy 4:7-8

Heaven: 2 Corinthians 5:1

Hell: 2 Thessalonians 1:9

Heresy and Dissent: Galatians 1:8-9; Colossians 2:8; Ephesians 4:14; 1 Timothy 1:3-7; 6:3-5; Titus 3:10-11

Hierarchy, Church: Ephesians 4:11-12

Holy Orders: Acts 13:3; 1 Timothy 4:14; 5:22; 2 Timothy 1:6

Incarnation of Christ: Philippians 2:1-11

Indulgences: 2 Corinthians 2:10

Inspiration of Scripture: 2 Timothy 3:16

Marriage, Sacramental: Romans 7:2-3; 1 Corinthians 7:10-11, 39; Ephesians 5:31; 1 Thessalonians 4:4

Mass, Obligation: 1 Corinthians 11:24-25

Mortal Sin: Romans 1:29-32; 1 Corinthians 6:9-10; Galatians 5:19-21; Ephesians 5:5

Original Sin: Romans 5:12-19; 1 Corinthians 15:21-22; Ephesians 2:3

Papacy: Galatians 1:17-19; 2:7-14

I am not ashamed of the gospel: it is the power of God for salvation to every one who has faith.

Romans 1:16

For we hold that a man is justified by faith apart from works of law.

Romans 3:28

The wages of sin is death.

Romans 6:23

I do not do the good I want, but the evil I do not want is what I do.

Romans 7:19

We do not know how to pray as we ought, but the Spirit himself intercedes for us with sighs too deep for words.

Romans 8:26

We know that in everything God works for good with those who love him.

Romans 8:28

If God is for us, who is against us?

Romans 8:31

Present your bodies as a living sacrifice, holy and acceptable to God, which is your spiritual worship.

Romans 12:1

Do not be conformed to this world but be transformed by the renewal of your mind.

Romans 12:2

Do not be overcome by evil, but overcome evil with good.

Romans 12:21

For the word of the cross is folly to those who are perishing, but to us who are being saved it is the power of God.

1 Corinthians 1:18

God chose what is foolish in the world to shame the wise, God chose what is weak in the world to shame the strong.

1 Corinthians 1:27

We are God's fellow workers.

1 Corinthians 3:9

For though absent in body I am present in spirit.

1 Corinthians 5:3

I have become all things to all men, that I might by all means save some.

1 Corinthians 9:22

Let any one who thinks that he stands take heed lest he fall.

1 Corinthians 10:12

If I speak in the tongues of men and of angels, but have not love, I am a noisy gong or a clanging cymbal. And if I have prophetic powers, and understand all mysteries and all knowledge, and if I have all faith, so as to remove mountains, but have not love, I am nothing. If I give away all I have, and if I deliver my body to be burned, but have not love, I gain nothing.

Love is patient and kind; love is not jealous or boastful; it is not arrogant or rude. Love does not insist on its own way; it is not irritable or resentful; it does not rejoice at wrong, but rejoices in the right. Love bears all things, believes all things, hopes all things, endures all things.

Love never ends; as for prophecies, they will pass away; as for tongues, they will cease; as for knowledge, it will pass away. For our knowledge is imperfect and our prophecy is imperfect; but when the perfect comes, the imperfect will pass away. When I was a child, I spoke like a child, I thought like a child, I reasoned like a child; when I became a man, I gave up childish ways. For now we see in a mirror dimly, but then face to face. Now I know in part; then I shall understand fully, even as I have been fully understood. So faith, hope, love abide, these three; but the greatest of these is love.

1 Corinthians 13:1-13

We walk by faith, not by sight.

2 Corinthians 5:7

[The Lord] said to me, "My grace is sufficient for you, for my power is made perfect in weakness."

2 Corinthians 12:9

It is no longer I who live, but Christ who lives in me.

Galatians 2:20

A little leaven leavens all the dough.

Galatians 5:9

Bear one another's burdens, and so fulfil the law of Christ.

Galatians 6:2

God is not mocked, for whatever a man sows, that he will also reap.

Galatians 6:7

[God] chose us in him before the foundation of the world, that we should be holy and blameless before him.

Ephesians 1:4

Put on the whole armor of God.

Ephesians 6:11

To live is Christ, and to die is gain.

Philippians 1:21

Work out your own salvation with fear and trembling.

Philippians 2:12

Whatever gain I had, I counted as loss for the sake of Christ.

Philippians 3:7

Whatever is true, whatever is honorable, whatever is just, whatever is pure, whatever is lovely, whatever is gracious, if there is any excellence, if there is anything worthy of praise, think about these things.

Philippians 4:8

I have learned, in whatever state I am, to be content. I know how to be abased, and I know how to abound.

Philippians 4:11-12

I can do all things in him who strengthens me.

Philippians 4:13

I complete what is lacking in Christ's afflictions for the sake of his body, that is, the Church.

Colossians 1:24

Your life is hidden with Christ in God.

Colossians 3:3

Pray constantly.

1 Thessalonians 5:17

Test everything; hold fast what is good.

1 Thessalonians 5:21

If any one will not work, let him not eat.

2 Thessalonians 3:10

The law is good, if any one uses it lawfully.

1 Timothy 1:8

Use a little wine for the sake of your stomach.

1 Timothy 5:23

Fight the good fight.

1 Timothy 6:12

I have fought the good fight, I have finished the race, I have kept the faith.

2 Timothy 4:7

To the pure all things are pure.

Titus 1:15

A Prayer to St. Paul
Glorious St. Paul, from being a persecutor of
the Christian name you became its most zealous Apostle. To make Jesus, our Divine Savior,
known to the uttermost parts of the earth you
suffered prison, scourgings, stonings, and
shipwreck, and all manner of persecutions,
and shed the last drop of your blood.

Obtain for us the grace to accept the infir-
mities, sufferings, and misfortunes of this life
as favors of divine mercy. So that we may
never grow weary of the trials of our exile, but
rather show ourselves ever more faithful and
fervent. Amen.

Litany of St. Paul the Apostle
Antiphon: You have searched me and known
me. You know when I sit and when I stand.

V. Great St. Paul, vessel of election, is
indeed worthy to be glorified.

R. *For he also deserved to possess the twelfth throne.*

V. Lord, have mercy.
R. *Christ, have mercy.*
V. Lord, have mercy.

Holy Mary, Mother of God...   *Pray for us.*
Queen conceived without original sin...
St. Paul...
Apostle of the Gentiles...
Vessel of Election...
St. Paul, you were rapt to the third heaven...
St. Paul, you heard things not given to man to utter...
St. Paul, you knew nothing but Christ, and him crucified...
St. Paul, your love for Christ was stronger than death...
St. Paul, you wished to be dissolved and be with Christ...
St. Paul, your zeal knew no bounds...
St. Paul, you made yourself all things to all, to gain all to Christ...

St. Paul, you called yourself prisoner of Christ for us... *Pray for us.*

St. Paul, you were jealous of us, with the jealousy of God...

St. Paul, you gloried only in the cross of Christ...

St. Paul, you bore in your body the dying of Christ...

St. Paul, you exclaimed: With Christ I am nailed to the cross!...

St. Paul, that we may awake and sin no more...

That we may not receive the grace of God in vain...

That we may walk in newness of life...

That we may work out our salvation with fear and trembling...

That we may put on the armor of God...

That we may stand against the deceits of the evil one...

That we may stand fast to the last...

That we may press forward to the mark...

That we may win the crown...

Lamb of God, who take away the sins of the
world...   *Spare us, O Lord.*
Lamb of God, who take away the sins of the
world...   *Graciously hear us, O Lord.*
Lamb of God, who take away the sins of the
world...   *Have mercy on us.*

Let us pray: O God, you who have taught the
whole world through the preaching of blessed
Paul the Apostle, grant that we, who celebrate
his memory, may, by following his example,
be drawn unto you. Through Our Lord Jesus
Christ your Son, who lives and reigns with
you in the unity of the Holy Spirit, God, for-
ever and ever. Amen.

9. For Further Reading

Gorman, Michael J., *Apostle of the Crucified Lord: A Theological Introduction to Paul and His Letters* (Grand Rapids, MI: Eerdmans, 2004).

———, *Reading Paul* (Eugene, OR: Cascade, 2007).

Hahn, Scott W., and Curtis Mitch, editors, *The Ignatius Catholic Study Bible: The Acts of the Apostles* (San Francisco: Ignatius Press, 2002).

———, *The Ignatius Catholic Study Bible: The Letter of Saint Paul to the Romans* (San Francisco: Ignatius Press, 2003).

———, *The Ignatius Catholic Study Bible: The First and Second Letters of Saint Paul to the Corinthians* (San Francisco: Ignatius Press, 2004).

———, *The Ignatius Catholic Study Bible: The Letters of Saint Paul to the Galatians and Ephesians* (San Francisco: Ignatius Press, 2005).

——— , *The Ignatius Catholic Study Bible: The Letters of Saint Paul to the Philippians, Colossians, and Philemon* (San Francisco: Ignatius Press, 2005).

——— , *The Ignatius Catholic Study Bible: The Letters of Saint Paul to the Thessalonians, Timothy, and Titus* (San Francisco: Ignatius Press, 2006).

Montague, George T., S.M., *The Living Thought of St. Paul* (Cincinnati: Benziger, 1976).

Pacwa, Mitch, S.J., *St. Paul: A Bible Study for Catholics* (Huntington, IN: Our Sunday Visitor, 2008).

Pimentel, Stephen, *Witnesses of the Messiah: On Acts of the Apostles 1-15* (Steubenville, OH: Emmaus Road, 2002).

——— , *Envoy of the Messiah: On Acts of the Apostles 16-28* (Steubenville, OH: Emmaus Road, 2005).

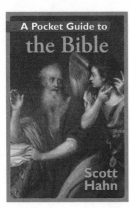